Seventy Selected Hadith From Al-Bukhari and Muslim

السَّبعُون المُختَارَة مِن الصَّحِيحَين

Compiled and Translated by

Dr. Abdossalam Salem Aboasha

د. عبدالسّلام سالم ابوعيشه

Seventy Selected Hadith from Al-Bukhari and Muslim

First Edition: 2017 – 1438
Printed in the United States of America

ISBN-13: 978-0-692-88142-2
ISBN-10: 0-692-88142-5

السَّبعُون المُختَارَة مِن الصَّحِيحَين
د. عبدالسّلام سالم ابوعيشه

الطّبعة الأولى: 2017-1438

Email: aa.aboasha@gmail.com
Telephone: (503)875-4604

بِسْمِ اللهِ الرَّحْمَـٰنِ الرَّحِيم

In the Name of Allah, the Most Gracious, the Most Merciful

In the Name of Allah, the Most Gracious, the Most Merciful

All praises are due to Allah. We praise Him, seek His help, His guidance, and ask for His forgiveness. We seek refuge with Allah from the evil within ourselves and from our sinful deeds. He, whom Allah guides, will never be misled and he whom He misguides, no one can guide. And I bear witness that there is no deity worthy of worship except Allah. And I bear witness that Muhammad is His servant and Messenger.

((O who you believe! Guard your duty to Allah and fear Him, and speak the truth. He will direct you to do good deeds and will forgive your sins. And whoever obeys Allah and His Messenger, he has won a great victory)) [33:70-71]. To proceed:

It has been narrated by at-Tirmidhi and others that the Prophet, peace be upon him, said: (May Allah make the face bright of whoever heard what I have said then learnt, memorized, and communicated it to others as it is. It may be that the recipient will understand it better than the one who has heard it).

In this book, I selected and translated seventy Hadith taking into account the following criteria:

1- The selected Ahadith should be authentic – selected from Sahih Al-Bukhari and/or Sahih Muslim.
2- The selected Ahadith should be short - easy to learn and memorize.
3- The selected Ahadith should include different topics.
4- All the words of the Ahadith should have harakat (vowel marks).
5- The English translation should be simple and easy.

I ask Allah, for help and guidance. Praise be to Almighty Allah, Lord of the worlds.

Dr. Abdossalam Salem Aboasha

7/2017 – 10/1438

بِسْمِ اللهِ الرَّحْمَٰنِ الرَّحِيم

إنَّ الْحَمْدَ لِلهِ ، نَحْمَدُهُ وَنَسْتَعِينُهُ وَنَسْتَغْفِرُهُ ، وَنَعُوذُ بِاللهِ مِنْ شُرُورِ أَنْفُسِنَا وَمِنْ سَيِّئَاتِ أَعْمَالِنَا ، مَنْ يَهْدِهِ اللهُ فَلا مُضِلَّ لَهُ، وَمَنْ يُضْلِلْ فَلا هَادِيَ لَهُ ، وَأَشْهَدُ أَنْ لَا إِلَهَ إِلَّا اللهُ وَحْدَهُ لَا شَرِيكَ لَهُ ، وَأَشْهَدُ أَنَّ مُحَمَّدًا عَبْدُهُ وَرَسُولُهُ.

((يَا أَيُّهَا الَّذِينَ آمَنُوا اتَّقُوا اللهَ وَقُولُوا قَوْلًا سَدِيدًا ، يُصْلِحْ لَكُمْ أَعْمَالَكُمْ وَيَغْفِرْ لَكُمْ ذُنُوبَكُمْ وَمَن يُطِعِ اللهَ وَرَسُولَهُ فَقَدْ فَازَ فَوْزًا عَظِيمًا)) [الأحزاب ، 70–71]. أَمَّا بَعْد:

لَقَدْ ثَبَتَ عَنِ النَّبِيِّ صَلَى اللهُ عَلَيْهِ وَسَلَم ، فِي سُنَنِ التِّرْمِذِي وَغَيْرِه أَنَّهُ قَالَ: (نَضَّرَ اللهُ امْرَأً سَمِعَ مَقَالَتِي فَوَعَاهَا وَحَفِظَهَا وَبَلَّغَهَا، فَرُبَّ حَامِلِ فِقْهٍ إِلَى مَنْ هُوَ أَفْقَهُ مِنْهُ).

وَعَلَيْهِ فَهَذِهِ سَبْعُونَ حَدِيثاً، أَرْجُو أَنْ تَكُونَ عَوْنًا لِطَلَبَةِ الْمَدَارِس وَلِمَنْ يَرْغَب فِي حِفْظِ الْحَدِيث، وَقَدْ قُمْتُ بِاخْتِيَارِهَا وتَرْجَمَتهَا وِفْقَ الشُّرُوطِ التَّالِيَة:

1. أنْ تَكُونَ الْأَحَادِيث صَحِيحَة - مَأْخُوذَة مِن الصَّحِيحَين (صَحِيحُ البُخَارِي وَ صَحِيحُ مُسْلِم أَوْ مِنْ أَحَدِهِمَا)
2. أنْ تَكُونَ الْأَحَادِيث قَصِيرَة - لِيَسْهُلَ حِفْظُهَا.
3. أنْ تَكُونَ الْأَحَادِيث مُتَنَوِّعَة – تَشْمُل كُلّ مَجَالَات الْحَيَاة.
4. أَنْ يَتِّمَ تَشْكِيل كُلّ كَلِمَات الْحَدِيث وَظَبْطهَا بِالْحَرَكَات.
5. أنْ تَكُونَ التَّرجَمَة - لِلُّغَةِ الْإنْجلِيزِيّة- بَسِيطَة وَسَهْلَة.

أَسْأَلُ اللهَ الْعَوْنَ وَالتَّوْفِيقَ وَآخِرُ دَعْوَانَا أَنِ الْحَمْدُ لِلهِ رَبِّ الْعَالَمِين.

د. عبدالسّلام سالم ابو عيشه

7/2017 – 10/1438

قَالَ اللهُ تَعَالَى:

(وَمَا آتَاكُمُ الرَّسُولُ فَخُذُوهُ وَمَا نَهَاكُمْ عَنْهُ فَانْتَهُوا وَاتَّقُوا اللهَ إِنَّ اللهَ شَدِيدُ الْعِقَابِ)

(And whatsoever the Messenger has given you, take it; and whatsoever he has forbidden you, refrain from it. And fear Allah; indeed, Allah is Severe in punishment)

(59:7)

[1]- الحَدِيثُ الأوَّل

عَنْ أَمِيرِ الْمُؤْمِنِينَ أَبِي حَفْصٍ عُمَرَ بْنِ الْخَطَّابِ، رَضِيَ اللهُ عَنْهُ، قَالَ: سَمِعْتُ رَسُولَ اللهِ صَلَّى اللهُ عَلَيْهِ وَسَلَّمَ يَقُولُ:

(إِنَّمَا الْأَعْمَالُ بِالنِّيَّاتِ، وَإِنَّمَا لِكُلِّ امْرِئٍ مَا نَوَى، فَمَنْ كَانَتْ هِجْرَتُهُ إِلَى اللهِ وَرَسُولِهِ فَهِجْرَتُهُ إِلَى اللهِ وَرَسُولِهِ، وَمَنْ كَانَتْ هِجْرَتُهُ لِدُنْيَا يُصِيبُهَا أَوِ امْرَأَةٍ يَنْكِحُهَا فَهِجْرَتُهُ إِلَى مَا هَاجَرَ إِلَيْهِ)

رَوَاهُ الْبُخَارِي ومُسْلِم.

The commander of the believers Umar bin Al-Khattab, may Allah be pleased with him, said: I heard the Messenger of Allah, Peace be upon him, saying:

(Actions are (judged) **by intentions, and everyone is rewarded according to his intention. Whoever has emigrated for Allah and His Messenger, his emigration will be for Allah and His Messenger; and whoever has emigrated for worldly benefit or to marry a woman, then his emigration is for what he has emigrated for)**

[Narrated by Al-Bukhari and Muslim].

[2] - الحَدِيثُ الثَّانِي

عَنْ أَبِي هُرَيْـرَةَ ، رَضِـيَ اللهُ عَنْـهُ ، قَالَ: قَالَ رَسُولُ اللهِ صَلَّى اللهُ عَلَيْهِ وَسَلَّمَ:

(إِنَّ اللهَ تَعَالَى لَا يَنْظُرُ إِلَى أَجْسَامِكُمْ ، وَلَا إِلَى صُوَرِكُمْ ، وَلَكِنْ يَنْظُرُ إِلَى قُلُوبِكُمْ وَأَعْمَالِكُمْ)

رَوَاهُ مُسْلِم.

Abu Hurairah, may Allah be pleased with him, said: The Messenger of Allah, peace be upon him said:

(The Almighty Allah does not look at your bodies or your images, but He looks at your hearts and your deeds)

[Narrated by Muslim].

[3] - الحَدِيثُ الثَّالِث

عَنِ ابْنِ عُمَرَ ، رَضِيَ اللهُ عَنْهُمَا ، قَالَ: قَالَ رَسُولُ اللهِ صَلَّى اللهُ عَلَيْهِ وَسَلَّمَ:

(بُنِيَ الْإِسْلَامُ عَلَى خَمْسٍ: شَهَادَةِ أَنْ لَا إِلَهَ إِلَّا اللهُ ، وَأَنَّ مُحَمَّدًا رَسُولُ اللهِ ، وَإِقَامِ الصَّلَاةِ ، وَإِيتَاءِ الزَّكَاةِ ، وَحَجِّ الْبَيْتِ ، وَصَوْمِ رَمَضَانَ)

رَوَاهُ البُخَارِي ومُسْلِم.

Ibin Umar, may Allah be pleased with them, said: The Messenger of Allah, peace be upon him, said:

(Islam is built on five pillars: testifying that there is no god but Allah, Muhammad is the Messenger of Allah, performing prayer, paying Zakat (obligatory charity), **performing pilgrimage to the House of Allah, and fasting the month of Ramadan)**

[Narrated by Al-Bukhari and Muslim].

[4] - الحَدِيثُ الرَّابِع

عَنْ عَبْدِاللهِ بْنِ مَسْعُودٍ ، رَضِيَ اللهُ عَنْهُ ، قَالَ: سَأَلْتُ النَّبِيَّ صَلَّى اللهُ عَلَيْهِ وَسَلَّمَ: أَيُّ الْعَمَلِ أَحَبُّ إِلَى اللهِ تَعَالَى؟ قَالَ:

(الصَّلَاةُ عَلَى وَقْتِهَا، قُلْتُ: ثُمَّ أَيٌّ؟ قَالَ: بِرُّ الْوَالِدَيْنِ، قُلْتُ : ثُمَّ أَيٌّ ؟ قَالَ: الْجِهَادُ فِي سَبِيلِ اللهِ)

رَوَاهُ الْبُخَارِي ومُسْلِم.

Abdu-Allah bin Mas'Uod, may Allah be pleased with him, said: I asked the Prophet, peace be upon him, which deeds are loved by Allah? He said:

(**Performing prayer on time,** I said then what? He said: **Honoring one's parents,** I said then what? He said: **Striving for the sake of Allah**)

[Narrated by Al-Bukhari and Muslim].

[5] - الحَدِيثُ الخَامِس

عَنِ ابْنِ عُمَرَ ، رَضِيَ اللهُ عَنْهُمَا ، أَنَّ رَسُولَ اللهِ صَلَّى اللهُ عَلَيْهِ وسَلَّمَ قَالَ:

(صَلَاةُ الْجَمَاعَةِ أَفْضَلُ مِنْ صَلَاةِ الْفَذِّ بِسَبْعٍ وَعِشْرِينَ دَرَجَةً)

رَوَاهُ الْبُخَارِي ومُسْلِم.

Ibin Umar, may Allah be pleased with them, reported that: The Messenger of Allah, peace be upon him, said:

(Prayer in congregation is better than praying alone by twenty-seven degrees)

[Narrated by Al-Bukhari and Muslim].

[6] - الحَدِيثُ السَّادِس

عَنْ أَبِي هُرَيْرَةَ ، رَضِيَ اللهُ عَنْهُ ، أَنَّ رَسُولَ اللهِ صَلَّى اللهُ عَلَيْهِ وَسَلَّمَ كَانَ يَقُولُ:

(الصَّلَوَاتُ الْخَمْسُ ، وَالْجُمُعَةُ إِلَى الْجُمُعَةِ ، وَرَمَضَانُ إِلَى رَمَضَانَ ، مُكَفِّرَاتٌ لِمَا بَيْنَهُنَّ إِذَا اجْتُنِبَتِ الْكَبَائِرُ)

رَوَاهُ مُسْلِمٌ.

Abu Hurairah, may Allah be pleased with him, reported that: The Messenger of Allah, peace be upon him, was saying:

(The five daily prayers and Friday to Friday and Ramadan to Ramadan is an expiation of sins to whom avoid major sins)

[Narrated by Muslim].

[7] - الحَدِيثُ السَّابِع

عَنْ أَبِي هُرَيْـرَةَ ، رَضِـيَ اللهُ عَنْهُ ، عَنِ النَّبِـيِّ صَلَّـى اللهُ عَلَيْـهِ وَسَلَّمَ قَالَ:

(مَـنْ صَامَ رَمَضَانَ إِيمَانًا وَاحْتِسَابًا غُفِرَ لَهُ مَا تَقَـدَّمَ مِـنْ ذَنْبِهِ)

رَوَاهُ البُخَارِي ومُسْلِم.

Abu Hurayrah, may Allah be pleased with him, reported that: The Prophet, peace be upon him, said:

(Whoever fasted the month of Ramadan out of faith and hope of reward from Allah, all his past sins will be forgiven)

[Narrated by Al-Bukhari and Muslim].

[8] - الحَدِيثُ الثَّامِن

عَنْ أَبِي هُرَيْـرَةَ ، رَضِـيَ اللهُ عَنْـهُ ، أَنَّ رَسُولَ اللهِ صَلَّى اللهُ عَلَيْهِ وَسَلَّمَ قَالَ:

(مَـنْ قَـامَ رَمَضَانَ إِيمَانًا وَاحْتِسَابًا غُفِـرَ لَـهُ مَا تَقَـدَّمَ مِـنْ ذَنْبِـهِ)

رَوَاهُ البُخَارِي ومُسْلِم.

Abu Hurairah, may Allah be pleased with him, reported that: The Messenger of Allah, peace be upon him, said:

(Whoever prayed at night (taraweeh prayer) **during Ramadan out of faith and hope of reward from Allah, all his past sins will be forgiven)**

[Narrated by Al-Bukhari and Muslim].

[9] - الحَدِيثُ التَّاسِع

عَنْ أَبِي هُرَيْرَةَ ، رَضِيَ اللهُ عَنْهُ ، عَنِ النَّبِيِّ صَلَّى اللهُ عَلَيْهِ وَسَلَّمَ قَالَ:

(مَنْ قَامَ لَيْلَةَ القَدْرِ إِيمَانًا وَاحْتِسَابًا غُفِرَ لَهُ مَا تَقَدَّمَ مِنْ ذَنْبِهِ)

رَوَاهُ البُخَارِي ومُسْلِم.

Abu Hurairah, may Allah be pleased with him, reported that: The Prophet, peace be upon him, said:

(Whoever prayed on the Night of Decree (Laila-tul Qadr) out of faith and hope of reward from Allah, all his past sins will be forgiven)

[Narrated by Al-Bukhari and Muslim].

[10] - الحَدِيثُ العَاشِر

عَنْ أُمِّ المُؤمِنِينَ ، أُمِّ عَبْدِاللهِ ، عَائِشَةَ رَضِيَ اللهُ عَنْهَا، أَنَّ رَسُولَ اللهِ صَلَّى اللهُ عَلَيْهِ وَسَلَّمَ قَالَ:

(تَحَرَّوْا لَيْلَةَ الْقَدْرِ فِي الْوِتْرِ مِنَ الْعَشْرِ الْأَوَاخِرِ مِنْ رَمَضَانَ)

رَوَاهُ البُخَارِي.

The mother of the believers, Aisha, may Allah be pleased with her, reported that: The Messenger of Allah, Peace be upon him, said:

(Search for the Night of Decree (Lailat-ul-Qadr) **on the odd nights of the last ten nights of Ramadan)**

[Narrated by Al-Bukhari].

[11] - الحَدِيثُ الحَادِي عَشَر

عَنْ أَبِي هُرَيْـرَةَ ، رَضِـيَ اللهُ عَنْـهُ ، قَالَ: سَمِعْتُ رَسُولَ اللهِ صَلَّـى اللهُ عَلَيْهِ وَسَلَّمَ يَقُولُ:

(مَنْ حَجَّ فَلَـمْ يَرْفُـثْ ، وَلَمْ يَفْسُـقْ ، رَجعَ كَيَـوْمِ وَلَدَتْـهُ أُمُّـهُ)

رَوَاهُ البُخَـارِي ومُسْلِم.

Abu Hurairah, may Allah be pleased with him said: I heard the Messenger of Allah, peace be upon him, saying:

(Whoever performs Hajj (pilgrimage) **and does not have sexual relations with his wife; does not commit sin, nor disputes, he returns from Hajj as the day he was born** (all his sins will be erased))

[Narrated by Al-Bukhari and Muslim].

[12] - الحَدِيثُ الثّانِي عشَر

عَنْ أَبِي هُرَيْـرَةَ ، رَضِـيَ اللهُ عَنْـهُ ، أَنَّ رَسُولَ اللهِ صَلَّى اللهُ عَلَيْهِ وَسَلَّمَ قَالَ:

(الْعُمْـرَةُ إِلَى الْعُمْـرَةِ كَفَّارَةٌ لِمَا بَيْنَهُمَا، وَالْحَجُّ الْمَبْـرُورُ لَيْسَ لَهُ جَـزَاءٌ إِلَّا الْجَنَّـةُ)

رَوَاهُ البُخَارِي ومُسْلِم.

Abu Hurairah, may Allah be pleased with him, reported that: The Messenger of Allah, peace be upon him, said:

(Umrah (minor pilgrimage) **to the next Umrah is an expiation of the sins committed between them, and the reward of accepted Hajj is nothing but Paradise)**

[Narrated by Al-Bukhari and Muslim].

[13] - الحَدِيثُ الثَّالِث عَشَر

عَنْ أُمِّ المُؤمِنِينَ ، أُمِّ عَبْدِاللهِ ، عَائِشَةَ رَضِيَ اللهُ عَنْهَا، قَالَتْ: قَالَ رَسُولُ اللهِ صَلَّى اللهُ عَلَيْهِ وَسَلَّمَ:

(مَنْ أَحْدَثَ فِي أَمْرِنَا هَذَا مَا لَيْسَ مِنْهُ فَهُوَ رَدٌّ)

رَوَاهُ البُخَارِي ومُسْلِم.

وَفِي رِوَايةٍ لِمُسْلِم:

(مَنْ عَمِلَ عَمَلًا لَيْسَ عَلَيْهِ أَمْرُنَا فَهُوَ رَدٌّ)

The mother of the believers, Aisha, may Allah be pleased with her, reported that: The Messenger of Allah, Peace be upon him, said:

(Whoever introduces to our matter (religion) **something that does not belong to it, it will be rejected)**

[Narrated by Al-Bukhari and Muslim].

The one reported by Muslim says:

(Whoever practices something that is not according to our matter (religion), **will be rejected)**

[14] - الحَدِيثُ الرَّابِع عَشَر

عَنْ أَبِي هُرَيْـرَةَ ، رَضِيَ اللهُ عَنْهُ ، أَنَّ رَسُولَ اللهِ صَلَّى اللهُ عَلَيْهِ وَسَلَّمَ قَالَ:

(كُلُّ أُمَّتِي يَدْخُلُونَ الْجَنَّةَ إِلَّا مَنْ أَبَى ، قَالُوا: يَا رَسُولَ اللهِ وَمَنْ يَأْبَى؟ قَالَ: **مَنْ أَطَاعَنِي دَخَلَ الْجَنَّةَ ، وَمَنْ عَصَانِي فَقَدْ أَبَى)**

رَوَاهُ البُخَارِي.

Abu Hurairah, may Allah be pleased with him, reported that: The Messenger of Allah, peace be upon him, said:

(All my Ummah (nation) **will enter Paradise except those who refuse,** He was asked: Who will refuse? He said: **Whoever obeys me will enter Paradise and whoever disobeys me, he refuses** (to enter Paradise))

[Narrated by Al-Bukhari].

[15] - الحَدِيثُ الخَامِس عَشَر

عَنْ أَبِي أُمَامَةَ ، رَضِيَ اللهُ عنهُ ، قَالَ: سَمِعْتُ رَسُولَ اللهِ صَلَّى اللهُ عَلَيْهِ وسَلَّمَ يَقُولُ:

(اِقْرَؤُوا الْقُرْآنَ فَإِنَّهُ يَأْتِي يَوْمَ الْقِيَامَةِ شَفِيعًا لِأَصْحَابِهِ)

رَوَاهُ مُسْلِمٌ.

Abu Umama, may Allah be pleased with him, said: I heard the Messenger of Allah, peace be upon him, saying:

(Read the Qur'an, because the Qur'an will come on the Day of Resurrection as an intercessor for its reciters)

[Narrated by Muslim].

[16] - الحَدِيثُ السَّادِس عَشَر

عَنْ عُثْمَانَ بْنِ عَفَّـانَ ، رَضِـيَ اللهُ عَنْـهُ ، قَالَ: قَالَ رَسُولُ اللهِ صَلَّـى اللهُ عَلَيْهِ وَسَلَّمَ:

(خَيْـرُكُمْ مَـنْ تَعَلَّـمَ الْقُـرْآنَ وَعَلَّمَـهُ)

رَوَاهُ الْبُخَـارِي.

Othman bin Affan, may Allah be pleased with him, said: The Messenger of Allah, peace be upon him, said:

(The best among you is the one who learns the Qur'an and teaches it to others)

[Narrated by Al-Bukhari].

[17] - الحَدِيثُ السَّابِع عَشَر

عَنْ أَنَسِ بْنِ مَالِكٍ ، رَضِيَ اللهُ عَنْهُ ، عَنِ النَّبِيِّ صَلَّى اللهُ عَلَيْهِ وَسَلَّمَ قَالَ:

(لَا يُؤْمِنُ أَحَدُكُمْ حَتَّى يُحِبَّ لِأَخِيهِ مَا يُحِبُّ لِنَفْسِهِ)

رَوَاهُ البُخَارِي ومُسْلِم.

Anas bin Malik, may Allah be pleased with him, reported that: The Prophet, peace be upon him, said:

(None of you believes until he loves for his brother what he loves for himself)

[Narrated by Al-Bukhari and Muslim].

[18] - الحَدِيثُ الثَّامِن عَشَر

عَنْ أَنَسٍ ، رَضِيَ اللهُ عَنْهُ ، عَنِ النَّبِيِّ صَلَّى اللهُ عَلَيْهِ وَسَلَّمَ قَالَ:

(لَا يُؤْمِنُ أَحَدُكُمْ حَتَّى أَكُونَ أَحَبَّ إِلَيْهِ مِنْ وَالِدِهِ ، وَوَلَدِهِ ، وَالنَّاسِ أَجْمَعِينَ)

رَوَاهُ البُخَارِي ومُسْلِم.

Anas, may Allah be pleased with him, reported that: The Prophet, peace be upon him, said:

(None of you believes until I am dearer to him than his father, his son, and all the people)

[Narrated by Al-Bukhari and Muslim].

[19] - الحَدِيثُ التَّاسِع عشَر

عَنْ أَبِي مُوسَى، رَضِيَ اللهُ عَنْهُ، قَالَ: قَالَ رَسُولُ اللهِ صَلَّى اللهُ عَلَيْهِ وَسَلَّمَ:

(الْمُؤْمِنُ لِلْمُؤْمِنِ كَالْبُنْيَانِ يَشُدُّ بَعْضُهُ بَعْضًا، وشَبَّكَ بَيْنَ أَصَابِعِه)

رَوَاهُ البُخَارِي ومُسْلِم.

Abu Musa, may Allah be pleased with him, said: The Messenger of Allah, peace be upon him, said:

(The believer to another believer is as bricks of a building, each one strengthens the other), and he clasped between his fingers.

[Narrated by Al-Bukhari and Muslim].

[20] - الحَدِيثُ الْعِشْرُون

عَنْ عَبْدِاللهِ بْنِ عَمْرٍو بْنِ الْعَاصِ، رَضِيَ اللهُ عَنْهُمَا، قَالَ: قَالَ رَسُولُ اللهِ صَلَّى اللهُ عَلَيْهِ وَسَلَّم:

(الْمُسْلِمُ مَنْ سَلِمَ الْمُسْلِمُونَ مِنْ لِسَانِهِ وَيَدِهِ، وَالْمُهَاجِرُ مَنْ هَجَرَ مَا نَهَى اللهُ عَنْهُ)

رَوَاهُ الْبُخَارِي ومُسْلِم.

Abdullah bin Amar, may Allah be pleased with him, reported that: The Messenger of Allah, peace be upon him, said:

(A Muslim is the one who does not harm Muslims with his tongue and/or his hand. And an emigrant is the one who does not do what Allah has forbidden)

[Narrated by Al-Bukhari and Muslim].

[21] - الحَدِيثُ الحَادِي وَالْعِشْرُون

عَنْ عُمَرَ بْنَ أَبِي سَلَمَةَ، رَضِيَ اللهُ عَنْهُمَا، قَالَ: كُنْتُ غُلاَمًا فِي حِجْرِ رَسُولِ اللهِ صَلَّى اللهُ عَلَيْهِ وَسَلَّمَ، وَكَانَتْ يَدِي تَطِيشُ فِي الصَّحْفَةِ، فَقَالَ لِي رَسُولُ اللهِ صَلَّى اللهُ عَلَيْهِ وَسَلَّمَ:

(يَا غُلاَمُ، سَمِّ اللهَ، وَكُلْ بِيَمِينِكَ، وَكُلْ مِمَّا يَلِيكَ)

رَوَاهُ البُخَارِي ومُسْلِم.

Umar ibn Abi Salamah, may Allah be pleased with them, said: I was a young boy under the care of the Messenger of Allah, peace be upon him, and my hands would wander in the dish, the Messenger of Allah, peace be upon him, said to me:

(O boy, say in the name of Allah, eat with your right hand, and eat from what is close to you)

[Narrated by Al-Bukhari and Muslim].

[22] - الحَدِيثُ الثَّانِي وَالْعِشْرُون

عَنْ جَابِرٍ ، رَضِيَ اللهُ عَنْهُ ، قَالَ: قَالَ رَسُولُ اللهِ صَلَّى اللهُ عَلَيْهِ وَسَلَّمَ:

(لَا تَأْكُلُوا بِالشِّمَالِ ؛ فَإِنَّ الشَّيْطَانَ يَأْكُلُ وَ يَشْرَبُ بِشِمَالِهِ)

رَوَاهُ مُسْلِمٌ.

Jabir, may Allah be pleased with them, reported that: The Messenger of Allah, peace be upon him, said:

(Do not eat with your left hand; because Satan eats and drinks with his left hand)

[Narrated by Muslim].

[23] - الحَدِيثُ الثَّالِثُ وَالْعِشْرُون

عَنْ أَبِي ذَرٍ، رَضِيَ اللهُ عَنْه، قَالَ: قَالَ لِي رَسُولُ اللهِ صَلَّى اللهُ عَلَيْهِ وَسَلَّمَ:

(لَا تَحْقِرَنَّ مِنَ الْمَعْرُوفِ شَيْئًا، وَلَوْ أَنْ تَلْقَى أَخَاكَ بِوَجْهٍ طَلِيقٍ)

رَوَاهُ مُسْلِم.

Abu Dhār, may Allah be pleased with him, said: The Messenger of Allah, peace be upon him, said to me:

(Do not belittle the good (deeds or acts)**, even if it is meeting your brother with a cheerful face)**

[Narrated by Muslim].

[24] - الحَدِيثُ الرَّابِعُ وَالْعِشْرُون

عَنْ عَدِيِّ بْنِ حَاتِمٍ ، رَضِيَ اللهُ عَنْهُ، قَالَ: سَمِعْتُ النَّبِيَّ صَلَّى اللهُ عَلَيْهِ وَسَلَّمَ يَقُولُ:

(اِتَّقُوا النَّارَ وَلَوْ بِشِقِّ تَمرَةٍ)

رَوَاهُ البُخَارِي ومُسْلِم.

Udia bin Hatim, may Allah be pleased with him, said: I heard the Prophet, peace be upon him, saying:

(Protect yourselves against Fire, even with half a date)

[Narrated by Al-Bukhari and Muslim].

[25] - الحَدِيثُ الخَامِسُ وَالْعِشْرُون

عَنْ مُعَاوِيَةَ ، رَضِيَ اللهُ عَنْهُ ، قَالَ: قَالَ رَسُولُ اللهِ صَلَّى للهُ عَلَيْهِ وسَلَّمَ:

(مَنْ يُرِدِ اللهُ بِهِ خَيْرًا يُفَقِّهْهُ فِي الدِّينِ)

رَوَاهُ البُخَارِي ومُسْلِم.

Mu-Awiyah, may Allah be pleased with him, said: The Messenger of Allah, peace be upon him, said:

(Whoever Allah wishes good for him, He gives him the understanding of religion)

[Narrated by Al-Bukhari and Muslim].

[26] - الحَدِيثُ السَّادِسُ وَالْعِشْرُون

عَنْ أَبِي هُرَيْرَةَ ، رَضِيَ اللهُ عَنْهُ ، أَنَّ رَسُولَ اللهِ صَلَّى اللهُ عَلَيْهِ وَسَلَّمَ قَالَ:

(مَنْ سَلَكَ طَرِيقًا يَلْتَمِسُ فِيهِ عِلْمًا سَهَّلَ اللهُ لَهُ بِهِ طَرِيقًا إِلَى الْجَنَّةِ)

رَوَاهُ مُسْلِمٌ.

Abu Hurairah, may Allah be pleased with him, reported that: The Messenger of Allah, peace be upon him, said:

(Whoever seeks a path to knowledge, Allah will ease his way to Paradise)

[Narrated by Muslim].

[27] - الحَدِيثُ السَّابِعُ وَالْعِشْرُون

عَنْ أَنَسٍ ، رَضِيَ اللهُ عَنْهُ ، أَنَّ رَسُولَ اللهِ صَلَّى اللهُ عَلَيْهِ وَسَلَّمَ قَالَ:

(مَنْ أَحَبَّ أَنْ يُبْسَطَ لَهُ فِي رِزْقِهِ ، وَيُنْسَأَ لَهُ فِي أَثَرِهِ ، فَلْيَصِلْ رَحِمَهُ)

رَوَاهُ الْبُخَارِي ومُسْلِم.

Anas, may Allah be pleased with him, reported that: The Messenger of Allah, peace be upon him, said:

(Whoever would like to increase his provisions and prolong his life, he should have good ties with his kinship)

[Narrated by Al-Bukhari and Muslim].

[28] - الحَدِيثُ الثَّامِنُ وَالْعِشْرُون

عَنْ أَبِي مَسْعُودٍ الأَنْصَارِيِّ الْبَدْرِيِّ، رَضِيَ اللهُ عَنْهُ، قَالَ: قَالَ رَسُولُ اللهِ صَلَّى اللهُ عَلَيْهِ وسَلَّم:

(مَنْ دَلَّ عَلَى خَيْرٍ فَلَهُ مِثْلُ أَجْرِ فَاعِلِهِ)

رَوَاهُ مُسْلِمٌ.

Abu Mas'ud al-Ansari al-Badri, may Allah be pleased with him, said: The Messenger of Allah, peace be upon him, said:

(Whoever guides others to goodness, he will be rewarded (by Allah) **similar to those who perform it)**

[Narrated by Muslim].

[29] - الحَدِيثُ التَّاسِعُ وَالْعِشْرُون

عَنْ أَبِي هُرَيْرَةَ ، رَضِيَ اللهُ عَنْهُ ، قَالَ: قَالَ رَسُولُ اللهِ صَلَّى اللهُ عَلَيْهِ وَسَلَّمَ:

(الدُّنْيَا سِجْنُ الْمُؤْمِنِ وَجَنَّةُ الْكَافِرِ)

رَوَاهُ مُسْلِمٌ.

Abu Hurairah, may Allah be pleased with him, said: The Messenger of Allah, peace be upon him, said:

(The life of this world is a prison for the believer and a Paradise for the disbeliever)

[Narrated by Muslim].

[30] - الحَدِيثُ الثَّلَاثُون

عَنْ أَبِي هُرَيْرَةَ ، رَضِيَ اللهُ عَنْهُ ، عَنْ رَسُولِ اللهِ صَلَّى اللهُ عَلَيْهِ وسَلَّمَ قَالَ:

(حُجِبَتِ النَّارُ بِالشَّهَوَاتِ ، وحُجِبَتِ الْجَنَّةُ بِالْمَكَارِهِ)

رَوَاهُ البُخَارِي ومُسْلِم.

Abu Hurairah, may Allah be pleased with him, reported that the Messenger of Allah, peace be upon him, said:

(The Fire is surrounded by desires, and Paradise is surrounded by hardships)

[Narrated by Al-Bukhari and Muslim].

[31] - الحَدِيثُ الحَادِي وَالثَّلاثُون

عَنْ عَائِشَةَ ، رَضِيَ اللهُ عَنْهَا ، قَالَتْ: قَالَ رَسُولُ اللهِ صَلَّى اللهُ عَلَيْهِ وَسَلَّمَ:

(إِنَّ اللهَ رَفِيقٌ يُحِبُّ الرِّفْقَ فِي الأَمْرِ كُلِّهِ)

رَوَاهُ البُخَارِي ومُسْلِم.

Aisha, may Allah be pleased with her, said: The Messenger of Allah, peace be upon him, said:

(Indeed, Allah is kind and He loves kindness in all matters)

[Narrated by Al-Bukhari and Muslim].

[32] - الحَدِيثُ الثَّانِي وَالثَّلَاثُون

عَنْ أَنَسٍ ، رَضِيَ اللهُ عَنْهُ ، عَنِ النَّبِيِّ صَلَّى اللهُ عَلَيْهِ وَسَلَّمَ قَالَ:

(يَسِّرُوا وَلَا تُعَسِّرُوا، وَبَشِّرُوا وَلَا تُنَفِّرُوا)

رَوَاهُ البُخَارِي ومُسْلِم.

Anas, may Allah be pleased with him, reported that: The Prophet, peace be upon him said:

(Facilitate things and do not make them difficult. Give people glad tidings and do not be repulsive)

[Narrated by Al-Bukhari and Muslim].

[33] - الحَدِيثُ الثَّالِثُ وَالثَّلاثُون

عَنْ أَبِي هُرَيْرَةَ ، رَضِيَ اللهُ عَنْهُ، أَنَّ رَسُولَ اللهِ صَلَّى اللهُ عَلَيْهِ وَسَلَّمَ قَالَ:

(لَيْسَ الشَّدِيدُ بِالصُّرْعَةِ ، إِنَّمَا الشَّدِيدُ الَّذِي يَمْلِكُ نَفْسَهُ عِنْدَ الْغَضَبِ)

رَوَاهُ البُخَارِي ومُسْلِم.

Abu Hurairah, may Allah be pleased with him, reported that: The Messenger of Allah, peace be upon him, said:

(The strong one is not who is a good wrestler, the strong one is who controls himself when he is angry)

[Narrated by Al-Bukhari and Muslim].

[34] - الحَدِيثُ الرَّابِعُ وَالثَّلَاثُون

عَنْ أَبِي هُرَيْرَةَ ، رَضِيَ اللهُ عَنْهُ ، أَنَّ رَجُلاً قَالَ: لِلنَّبِيِّ صَلَّى اللهُ عَلَيْهِ وسَلَّمَ أوْصِنِي ، قَالَ:

(لَا تَغْضَبْ ، فَرَدَّدَ مِرَارًا ، قَالَ: لَا تَغْضَبْ)

رَوَاهُ. البُخَارِيُّ.

Abu Hurairah, may Allah be pleased with him, reported that: a man said to the Prophet, peace be upon him, advise me, The Prophet said:

(Do not get angry, the man repeated his request for advice, **He** (The Prophet) **said**: **do not get angry)**

[Narrated by Al-Bukhari].

[35] - الحَدِيثُ الخَامِسُ وَالثَّلَاثُون

عَنْ أَبِي مُوسَى الْأَشْعَرِيِّ، رَضِيَ اللهُ عَنْهُ، عَنِ النَّبِيِّ صَلَّى اللهُ عَلَيْهِ وسَلَّمَ قَالَ:

(إِنَّ اللهَ تَعَالَى يَبْسُطُ يَدَهُ بِاللَّيْلِ لِيَتُوبَ مُسِيءُ النَّهَارِ، وَيَبْسُطُ يَدَهُ بِالنَّهَارِ لِيَتُوبَ مُسِيءُ اللَّيْلِ، حَتَّى تَطْلُعَ الشَّمْسُ مِنْ مَغْرِبِهَا)

رَوَاهُ مُسْلِمٌ.

Abu Musa Al-Ash'ari, may Allah be pleased with him, reported that: The Prophet, peace be upon him, said:

(Verily, the Almighty Allah, stretches out His Hand at night, so that the sinners of the day may repent, and stretches out His Hand during the day so that the sinners of the night may repent. He continuously does so until the sun rises from the west)

[Narrated by Muslim].

[36] - الحَدِيثُ السَّادِسُ وَالثَّلَاثُون

عَنْ أَبِي هُرَيْرَةَ ، رَضِيَ اللهُ عَنْهُ ، قَالَ: قَالَ رَسُولُ اللهِ صَلَّى اللهُ عَلَيْهِ وَسَلَّمَ:

(مَنْ تَابَ قَبْلَ أَنْ تَطْلُعَ الشَّمْسُ مِنْ مَغْرِبِهَا، تَابَ اللهُ عَلَيْهِ)

رَوَاهُ مُسْلِمٌ.

Abu Hurairah, may Allah be pleased with him, said: The Messenger of Allah, peace be upon him said:

(Whoever repents before the sun rises from the west, Allah will accept his repentance (will forgive him))

[Narrated by Muslim].

[37] - الحَدِيثُ السَّابِعُ وَالثَّلاثُون

عَنْ أَبِي هُرَيْـرَةَ ، رَضِـيَ اللهُ عَنْهُ ، قَالَ: قَالَ رَسُولُ اللهِ صَلَّى اللهُ عَلَيْهِ وَسَلَّمَ:

(كَلِمَتَانِ خَفِيفَتَانِ عَلَى اللِّسَانِ ، ثَقِيلَتَـانِ فِي الْمِيزَانِ ، حَبِيبَتَانِ إِلَى الرَّحْمَٰنِ ، سُبْحَانَ اللهِ وَبِحَمْدِهِ ، سُبْحَانَ اللهِ الْعَظِيمِ)

رَوَاهُ البُخَارِي ومُسْلِم.

Abu Hurairah, may Allah be pleased with him, said: The Messenger of Allah, peace be upon him, said:

(Two words are light on the tongue, heavy on the scale, and dear to the Merciful: Praise be to Allah Almighty, Glory and praise be to Allah)

[Narrated by Al-Bukhari and Muslim].

[38] - الحَدِيثُ الثَّامِنُ وَالثَّلَاثُون

عَنْ عَبْدِاللهِ بْنِ عَمْرِو بْنِ العَاصِ ، رَضِيَ اللهُ عَنْهُمَا، أَنَّهُ سَمِعَ رَسُولَ اللهِ صَلَّى اللهُ عَلَيْهِ وَسَلَّمَ يَقُولُ:

(مَنْ صَلَّى عَلَيَّ صَلَاةً صَلَّى اللهُ عَلَيْهِ بِهَا عَشْرًا)

رَوَاهُ مُسْلِمٌ.

Abdullah ibn Amar ibn Al-Aas, may Allah be pleased with them, said: I heard the Messenger of Allah, peace be upon him, saying:

(Whoever prays on me one time, Allah will pray on him ten times)

[Narrated by Muslim].

[39] - الحَدِيثُ التَّاسِعُ وَالثَّلَاثُون

عَنْ أَبِي هُرَيْـرَةَ ، رَضِـيَ اللهُ عَنْهُ ، قَالَ: قَالَ رَسُولُ اللهِ صَلَّى اللهُ عَلَيْهِ وَسَلَّمَ:

(إِذَا مَاتَ ابْنُ آدَمَ انْقَطَعَ عَمَلُهُ إِلَّا مِـنْ ثَلَاثٍ: صَدَقَـةٍ جَارِيَـةٍ ، أَوْ عِلْمٍ يُنْتَـفَعُ بِهِ ، أَوْ وَلَـدٍ صَالِحٍ يَدْعُو لَهُ)

رَوَاهُ مُسْلِمٌ.

Abu Hurairah, may Allah be pleased with him, said: The Messenger of Allah, peace be upon him, said:

(If the son of Adam dies, then his actions come to an end except for three: ongoing charity, beneficial knowledge, or a righteous child who prays for him)

[Narrated by Muslim].

[40] - الحَدِيثُ الأَرْبَعُون

عَنْ جَـابِرٍ، رَضِيَ اللهُ عَنْهُ ، قَالَ: جَاءَ أَعْرَابِيٌّ إِلَى النَّبِيِّ صَلَّى اللهُ عَلَيْهِ وَسَلَّمَ ، فقَالَ: يَا رَسُولَ اللهِ ، مَا الْمُوجِبَتَانِ ؟ فَقَالَ:

(مَـنْ مَاتَ لَا يُشْرِكُ بِاللهِ شَيْـئًا دَخَـلَ الْجَنَّةَ ، وَمَـنْ مَاتَ يُشْرِكُ بِهِ شَيْئًا دَخَلَ النَّـارَ)

رَوَاهُ مُسْلِمٌ.

Jabir, may Allah be pleased with him, said: A Bedouin came to the Prophet, peace be upon him, and said: O Messenger of Allah, what are the two mandates? He (The Prophet) said:

(Whoever dies and does not associate anything with Allah, he will enter Paradise and whoever dies associating anything with Him, he will enter Fire)

[Narrated by Muslim].

[41] - الحَدِيثُ الحَادِي وَالأَرْبَعُون

عَنِ النَّوَّاسِ بْنِ سَمْعَانَ ، رَضِيَ اللهُ عَنْهُ، عَنِ النَّبِيِّ صَلَّى اللهُ عَلَيْهِ وسَلَّمَ قَالَ:

(الْبِرُّ حُسْنُ الْخُلُقِ ، وَالْإِثْمُ مَا حَاكَ فِي نَفْسِكَ، وكَرِهْتَ أَنْ يَطَّلِعَ عَلَيْهِ النَّاسُ)

رَوَاهُ مُسْلِمٌ.

Annawas bin Samaan, may Allah be pleased with him, reported that: The Prophet, peace be upon him, said:

(Righteousness is good morality. The sin is what creates doubt in yourself and you do not want people to know about)

[Narrated by Muslim].

[42] - الحَدِيثُ الثَّانِي وَالأرْبَعُون

عَنْ عَبْدِ اللهِ بْنِ عَمْرٍو بْنِ الْعَاصِ، رَضِيَ اللهُ عَنْهُمَا، قَالَ: لَمْ يَكُنْ رَسُولُ اللهِ صَلَّى اللهُ عَلَيْهِ وَسَلَّمَ، فَاحِشًا وَلَا مُتَفَحِّشًا وَكَانَ يَقُولُ:

(إِنَّ مِنْ خِيَارِكُمْ أَحْسَنَكُمْ أَخْلَاقًا)

رَوَاهُ البُخَارِي ومُسْلِم.

Abdullah ibn Amr ibn Al-Aas, may Allah be pleased with him, said the Messenger of Allah, peace be upon him, was not obscene nor did he like listening to it, and he used to say:

(Indeed, the best among you is the one who has the best manners)

[Narrated by Al-Bukhari and Muslim].

[43] - الحَدِيثُ الثَّالِثُ وَالأَرْبَعُون

عَنْ عَبْدِ اللهِ بْنِ عَمْرِو بْنِ الْعَاصِ، رَضِيَ اللهُ عَنْهُمَا، أَنَّ رَجُلاً سَأَلَ رَسُولَ اللهِ صَلَّى اللهُ عَلَيْهِ وسَلَّمَ: أَيُّ الْإِسْلَامِ خَيْرٌ ؟ قَالَ:

(تُطْعِمُ الطَّعَامَ، وَتَقْرَأُ السَّلَامَ، عَلَى مَنْ عَرَفْتَ وَمَنْ لَمْ تَعْرِفْ)

رَوَاهُ البُخَارِي ومُسْلِم.

Abdullah ibn Amr ibn Al-Aas, may Allah be pleased with them, reported that: a man asked the Messenger of Allah, peace be upon him, which act is the best in Islam? He said:

(To feed the needy and to greet (say Salaam) **to the one you know and to the one you do not know)**

[Narrated by Al-Bukhari and Muslim].

[44] - الحَدِيثُ الرَّابِعُ وَالأَرْبَعُون

عَنْ أَبِي هُرَيْرَةَ ، رَضِيَ اللهُ عَنْهُ، عَنِ النَّبِيِّ صَلَّى اللهُ عَلَيْهِ وَسَلَّمَ قَالَ:

(مَنْ كَانَ يُؤْمِنُ بِاللهِ وَالْيَوْمِ الآخِرِ فَلْيَقُلْ خَيْرًا ، أَوْ لِيَصْمُتْ)

رَوَاهُ البُخَارِي ومُسْلِم.

Abu Hurairah, may Allah be pleased with him, reported that: The Prophet, peace be upon him, said:

(Whoever believes in Allah and the Last Day (Hereafter)**, let him speak well or remain silent)**

[Narrated by Al-Bukhari and Muslim].

[45] - الحَدِيثُ الخَامِسُ وَالأَرْبَعُون

عَنْ أَبِي هُرَيْرَةَ، رَضِيَ اللهُ عَنْهُ، قَالَ: قَالَ رَسُولُ اللهِ صَلَّى اللهُ عَلَيْهِ وَسَلَّمَ:

(خَيْرُ يَوْمٍ طَلَعَتْ عَلَيْهِ الشَّمْسُ يَوْمُ الْجُمُعَةِ: فِيهِ خُلِقَ آدَمُ، وَفِيهِ أُدْخِلَ الْجَنَّةَ، وَفِيهِ أُخْرِجَ مِنْهَا)

رَوَاهُ مُسْلِمٌ.

Abu Hurairah, may Allah be pleased with him, said: The Messenger of Allah, peace be upon him, said:

(The best day on which the sun rises is Friday: on this day Adam was created, on this day he entered Paradise, and on this day he got out of Paradise)

[Narrated by Muslim].

[46] - الحَدِيثُ السَّادِسُ وَالأَرْبَعُون

عَنْ أَبِي قَتَادَةَ ، رَضِيَ اللهُ عَنْهُ ، قَالَ: سُئِلَ رَسُولُ اللهِ صَلَّى اللهُ عَلَيْهِ وسَلَّم: عَنْ صَوْمِ يَـوْمِ عَرَفَةَ ؟ قَالَ:

(يُكَفِّرُ السَّـنَةَ الْمَاضِيَةَ وَ الْبَاقِيَـةَ)

رَوَاهُ مُسْلِمٌ.

Abu Qatada, may Allah be pleased with him, said: the Messenger of Allah, peace be upon him, has been asked about fasting on the Day of Arafat, he said:

(It (the Day of Arafat) **expiates the sins of the past year and the coming year)**

[Narrated by Muslim].

[47] - الحَدِيثُ السَّابِعُ وَالأرْبَعُون

عَنْ بُرَيْدَةَ ، رَضِيَ اللهُ عَنْهُ ، قَالَ: قَالَ رَسُولُ اللهِ صَلَّى اللهُ عَلَيْهِ وسَلَّمَ:

(كُنْتُ نَهَيْتُكُمْ عَنْ زِيَارَةِ الْقُبُورِ فَزُورُوهَا)

رَوَاهُ مُسْلِمٌ.

Buraydah, may Allah be pleased with him, said: The Messenger of Allah, peace be upon him, said:

(I have forbidden you to visit graves, but now visit them)

[Narrated by Muslim].

[48] - الحَدِيثُ الثَّامِنُ وَالأرْبَعُون

عَنْ أَبِي مَرْثَدٍ كَنَّازِ بْنِ الْحُصَيْنِ، رَضِيَ اللهُ عَنْهُ، قَالَ: سَمِعْتُ رَسُولَ اللهِ صَلَّى اللهُ عَلَيْهِ وسَلَّم يَقُولُ:

(لَا تُصَلُّوا إِلَى الْقُبُورِ، وَلَا تَجْلِسُوا عَلَيْهَا)

رَوَاهُ مُسْلِمٌ.

Abu Marthad Knaaz bin Al-Husain, may Allah be pleased with him, said: I heard the Messenger of Allah, peace be upon him, saying:

(Do not pray towards the graves, and do not sit on them)

[Narrated by Muslim].

[49] - الحَدِيثُ التَّاسِعُ وَالأَرْبَعُون

عَنْ أَبِي عِيسَى الْمُغِيرَةِ بْنِ شُعْبَةَ ، رَضِيَ اللهُ عَنْهُ، عَنِ النَّبِيِّ صَلّى اللهُ عَلَيْهِ وسَلَّمَ قَالَ:

(إِنَّ اللهَ تَعَالَى حَرَّمَ عَلَيْكُمْ عُقُوقَ الْأُمَّهَاتِ ، وَمَنْعًا وَهَاتِ ، وَوَأْدَ الْبَنَاتِ ، وَكَرِهَ لَكُمْ قِيلَ وَقَالَ ، وَكَثْرَةَ السُّؤَالِ ، وَإِضَاعَةَ الْمَالِ)

رَوَاهُ الْبُخَارِي ومُسْلِم.

Abu-Isa Al-Mughirah bin Shuabah, may Allah be pleased with him, reported that: The Prophet, peace be upon him, said:

(Allah has forbidden for you: disobedience to your mothers, to withhold (what you should give)**, demand** (what you do not deserve)**, and to bury your daughters alive. And Allah dislikes useless talk, asking too many questions** (that have no benefit)**, and wasting your wealth)**

[Al-Bukhari and Muslim].

[50] - الحَدِيثُ الخَمْسُون

عَنْ عَبْدِ اللهِ بْنِ عَمْرِو بْنِ الْعَاصِ، رَضِيَ اللهُ عَنْهُمَا، عَنِ النَّبِيِّ صَلَّى اللهُ عَلَيْهِ وسَلَّمَ قَالَ:

(الْكَبَائِـرُ: الْإِشْـرَاكُ بِاللهِ ، وَعُقُـوقُ الْوَالِدَيْـنِ ، وقَتْـلُ النَّفْسِ ، والْيَمِينُ الْغَمُوسُ)

رَوَاهُ الْبُخَارِي.

Abdullah bin Amr bin Al-As, may Allah be pleased with them, reported that: The Prophet, peace be upon him, said:

(The major sins are: to ascribe partners to Allah, to disobey parents, to murder someone, and to take a false oath (intentionally)**)**

[Narrated by Al-Bukhari].

[51] - الحَدِيثُ الحَادِي وَالخَمْسُون

عَنْ أَبِي سَعِيدٍ الخُدْرِيِّ ، رَضِيَ اللهُ عَنْهُ ، قَالَ: سَمِعْتُ رَسُولَ اللهِ صَلَّى اللهُ عَلَيْهِ وَسَلَّمَ يَقُولُ:

(مَنْ رَأَى مِنْكُمْ مُنْكَرًا فَلْيُغَيِّرْهُ بِيَدِهِ ، فَإِنْ لَمْ يَسْتَطِعْ فَبِلِسَانِهِ ، فَإِنْ لَمْ يَسْتَطِعْ فَبِقَلْبِهِ وَذَلِكَ أَضْعَفُ الإِيمَانِ)

رَوَاهُ مُسْلِمٌ.

Abu Sa`id Al-Khudri, may Allah be pleased with him, reported that: The Messenger of Allah, peace be upon him, said:

(Whoever among you who sees an evil act, must change it with his hand; if he cannot do so, then with his tongue; and if he cannot do so, then with his heart; and that is the weakest form of faith)

[Narrated by Muslim].

[52] - الحَدِيثُ الثَّانِي وَالخَمْسُون

عَنْ جَابِرٍ رَضِيَ اللهُ عَنْهُ ، أَنَّ رَسُولَ اللهِ صَلَّى اللهُ عَلَيْهِ وسَلَّمَ قَالَ:

(اتَّقُوا الظُّلْمَ ، فَإِنَّ الظُّلْمَ ظُلُمَاتٌ يَوْمَ القِيامَةِ، وَاتَّقُوا الشُّحَّ ، فَإِنَّ الشُّحَّ أَهْلَكَ مَنْ كَانَ قَبْلَكُمْ، حَمَلَهُم عَلَى أَنْ سَفَكُوا دِمَاءَهُمْ وَاسْتَحَلُّوا مَحَارِمَهُمْ)

رَوَاهُ مُسْلِمٌ.

Jabir, may Allah be pleased with him, reported that: The Messenger of Allah, peace be upon him, said:

(Beware of injustice because injustice will be darkness on the Day of Resurrection; and beware of stinginess because it has destroyed those who were before you. It led them to shed their blood and consider what is unlawful as lawful)

[Narrated by Muslim].

[53] - الحَدِيثُ الثَّالِثُ وَالخَمسُون

عَنْ صَفِيَّـةَ بِنْتِ أَبِي عُبَيْدٍ ، رَضِيَ اللهُ عَنْهَا ، عَنْ بَعْضِ أَزْوَاجِ النَّبِيِّ ، رَضِيَ اللهُ عَنْهُمْ ، عَنِ النَّبِيِّ صَلَّى اللهُ عَلَيْهِ وَسَلَّمَ قَالَ:

(مَـنْ أَتَى عَرَّافًا فَسَأَلَهُ عَـنْ شَىْءٍ ، فَصَدَّقَهُ ، لَمْ تُقْبَـلْ لَـهُ صَلَاةٌ أَرْبَعِيـنَ يَوْمًا)

رَوَاهُ مُسْلِمٌ.

Safiyyah, daughter of Abu-Ubaid, may Allah be pleased with her, on the authority of some of the wives of the Prophet, may Allah be pleased with them all, they said: The Messenger of Allah, peace be upon him, said:

(Whoever goes to a fortune-teller and asks him about something then believes him, his prayer will not be accepted for forty days)

[Narrated by Muslim].

[54] - الحَدِيثُ الرَّابِعُ وَالخَمْسُون

عَنْ أَبِي هُرَيْرَةَ، رَضِيَ اللهُ عَنْهُ، أَنَّ رَسُولَ اللهِ صَلَّى اللهُ عَلَيْهِ وَسَلَّمَ قَالَ:

(آيَةُ الْمُنَافِقِ ثَلَاثٌ: إِذَا حَدَّثَ كَذَبَ، وَإِذَا وَعَدَ أَخْلَفَ، وَإِذَا اؤْتُمِنَ خَانَ)

رَوَاهُ البُخَارِي ومُسْلِم.

Abu Hurairah, may Allah be pleased with him, reported that: The Messenger of Allah, peace be upon him, said:

(There are three signs of a hypocrite: When he speaks; he lies; when he makes a promise, he breaks it; and when he is trusted, he betrays that trust)

[Al-Bukhari and Muslim].

[55] - الحَدِيثُ الخَامِسُ وَالخَمْسُون

عَنْ أَبِي هُرَيْرَةَ ، رَضِيَ اللهُ عَنْهُ ، أَنَّ رَسُولَ اللهِ صَلَّى اللهُ عَلَيْهِ وَسَلَّمَ قَالَ:

(كَانَ رَجُلٌ يُدَايِنُ النَّاسَ ، وَكَانَ يَقُولُ لِفَتَاهُ: إِذَا أَتَيْتَ مُعْسِرًا فَتَجَاوَزْ عَنْهُ ، لَعَلَّ اللهَ أنْ يَتَجَاوَزَ عَنَّا ، فَلَقِيَ اللهَ فَتَجَاوَزَ عَنْهُ)

رَوَاهُ البُخَارِي ومُسْلِم.

Abu Hurairah, may Allah be pleased with him, reported that: The Messenger of Allah, peace be upon him, said:

(There was a person who used to loan money to the people and he used to say to his servant, "If the borrower is unable to pay, forgive him, so that Allah may forgive us." So when he met Allah (when he died), **Allah forgave him)**

[Al-Bukhari and Muslim].

[56] - الحَدِيثُ السَّادِسُ وَالخَمْسُون

عَنْ أَبِي هُرَيْرَةَ ، رَضِيَ اللهُ عَنْهُ ، أَنَّ رَسُولَ اللهِ صَلَّى اللهُ عَلَيْهِ وَسَلَّمَ قَالَ:

(مَا نَقَصَتْ صَدَقَةٌ مِنْ مَالٍ ، وَمَا زَادَ اللهُ عَبْدًا بِعَفْوٍ إِلَّا عِزًّا، وَمَا تَوَاضَعَ أَحَدٌ لِلهِ إِلَّا رَفَعَهُ اللهُ عَزَّ وَجَلَّ)

رَوَاهُ مُسْلِمٌ.

Abu Hurairah, may Allah be pleased with him, reported: The Messenger of Allah, peace be upon him, said:

(Wealth is not decreased by giving charity. Allah will honor the one who forgives; and Allah will raise the rank of those who are humble)

[Narrated by Muslim].

[57] - الحَدِيثُ السَّابِعُ وَالخَمْسُون

عَنْ أَبِي هُرَيْرَةَ ، رَضِيَ اللهُ عَنْهُ ، قَالَ: قَالَ رَسُولُ اللهِ صَلَّى اللهُ عَلَيْهِ وسَلَّمَ:

(وَالَّذِي نَفْسِي بِيَدِهِ لَا تَدْخُلُوا الْجَنَّةَ حَتَّى تُؤْمِنُوا وَلَا تُؤْمِنُوا حَتَّى تَحَابُّوا ، أَوَلَا أَدُلُّكُمْ عَلَى شَيْءٍ إِذَا فَعَلْتُمُوهُ تَحَابَبْتُمْ ؟ أَفْشُوا السَّلَامَ بَيْنَكُمْ)

رَوَاهُ مُسْلِمٌ.

Abu Hurairah, may Allah be pleased with him, reported that: The Messenger of Allah, peace be upon him, said:

(By Him in Whose Hand my soul is! You will not enter Paradise until you believe, and you shall not believe until you love one another. May I inform you of something, if you do it, you would love each other? Spread greeting (saying Assalamu Alaikum) **among yourselves)**

[Narrated by Muslim].

[58] - الحَدِيثُ الثَّامِنُ وَالخَمْسُون

عَنْ أَبِي هُرَيْـرَةَ ، رَضِـيَ اللهُ عَنْهُ ، عَنِ النَّبِيِّ صَلَّى اللهُ عَلَيْهِ وَسَلَّمَ قَالَ:

(لَا يَسْتُرُ عَبْدٌ عَبْدًا فِي الدُّنْيَا ، إِلَّا سَتَرَهُ اللهُ يَـوْمَ الْقِيَامَةِ)

رَوَاهُ مُسْلِمٌ.

Abu Hurairah, may Allah be pleased with him, reported that: The Prophet, peace be upon him, said:

(Whoever covers up the faults of others in this world, Allah will cover up his faults on the Day of Resurrection)

[Narrated by Muslim].

[59] - الحَدِيثُ التَّاسِعُ وَالخَمْسُون

عَنْ أَبِي أَيُّوبَ ، رَضِيَ اللهُ عَنْهُ ، أَنَّ رَسُولَ اللهِ صَلَّى اللهُ عَلَيْهِ وسَلَّمَ قَالَ:

(لَا يَحِلُّ لِمُسْلِمٍ أَنْ يَهْجُرَ أَخَاهُ فَوْقَ ثَلَاثِ لَيَالٍ: يَلْتَقِيَانِ ، فَيُعْرِضُ هَذَا ويُعْرِضُ هَذَا ، وخَيْرُهُمَا الَّذِي يَبْدَأُ بِالسَّلَامِ)

رَوَاهُ البُخَارِي ومُسْلِم.

Abu Ayyub Al-Ansari, may Allah be pleased with him, said: The Messenger of Allah, peace be upon him, said:

(It is unlawful for a Muslim to stop talking to his brother beyond three nights. They meet, but each one turns away from the other. And the best of the two is the one who greets the other first)

[Al-Bukhari and Muslim].

[60] - الحَدِيثُ السِّتُّون

عَنْ أَبِي هُرَيْرَةَ ، رَضِيَ اللهُ عَنْهُ ، أَنَّ رَسُولَ اللهِ صَلَّى اللهُ عَلَيْهِ وَسَلَّمَ قَالَ:

(بِحَسْبِ امْرِئٍ مِنَ الشَّرِّ أَنْ يَحْقِرَ أَخَاهُ المُسْلِمَ)

رَوَاهُ مُسْلِمٌ.

Abu Hurairah, may Allah be pleased with him, said: The Messenger of Allah, peace be upon him said:

(It is enough evil for a Muslim to despise his Muslim brother)

[Narrated by Muslim].

[61] - الحَدِيثُ الحَادِي وَالسِّتُّون

عَنْ أَبِي هُرَيْـرَةَ ، رَضِـيَ اللهُ عَنْهُ، عَنِ النَّبِيِّ صَلَّى اللهُ عَلَيْهِ وَسَلَّمَ قَالَ:

(تُـنْكَحُ الْمَـرْأَةُ لِأَرْبَـعٍ: لِمَـالِهَا ، وَلِحَسْبِهَا ، وَلِجَمَالِهَا ، وَلِدِينِهَا ، فَاظْفَرْ بِذَاتِ الدِّينِ تَرِبَتْ يَـدَاكَ)

رَوَاهُ البُخَارِي ومُسْلِم.

Abu Hurairah, may Allah be pleased with him, reported that: The Prophet, peace be upon him, said:

(A woman is married for four reasons: for her wealth, for her family status, for her beauty, and for her religion. Choose the religious woman, may you be blessed)

[Al-Bukhari and Muslim].

[62] - الحَدِيثُ الثَّانِي وَالسِّتُّون

عَنْ عَبْدِ اللهِ بْنِ عَمْرِو بْنِ الْعَاصِ، رَضِيَ اللهُ عَنْهُمَا، أَنَّ رَسُولَ اللهِ صَلَّى اللهُ عَلَيْهِ وسَلَّمَ قَالَ:

(الدُّنْيَا مَتَاعٌ ، وَخَيْرُ مَتَاعِهَا الْمَرْأَةُ الصَّالِحَةُ)

رَوَاهُ مُسْلِمٌ.

Abdullah bin Amr bin Al-As, may Allah be pleased with them, reported that: The Messenger of Allah, peace be upon him, said:

(The world (this life) **is but an enjoyment; and the best enjoyment of this world is a pious and virtuous woman)**

[Narrated by Muslim].

[63] - الحَدِيثُ الثَّالِثُ وَالسِّتُّون

عَنِ ابْنِ عُمَرَ وَعَائِشَةَ ، رَضِيَ اللهُ عَنْهُمَا ، قَالَا: قَالَ رَسُولُ اللهِ صَلَّى اللهُ عَلَيْهِ وسَلَّمَ:

(مَا زَالَ جِبْرِيلُ يُوصِينِي بِالْجَارِ حَتَّى ظَنَنْتُ أَنَّهُ سَيُوَرِّثُهُ)

رَوَاهُ البُخَارِي ومُسْلِم.

Ibn Umar and Aisha, may Allah be pleased with them, reported that: The Messenger of Allah, peace be upon him, said:

(Gabriel kept recommending me to be nice to the neighbors, so much so that I thought he would assign them a share of inheritance)

[Al-Bukhari and Muslim].

[64] - الحَدِيثُ الرَّابِعُ وَالسِّتُّون

عَنْ أَبِي هُرَيْرَةَ ، رَضِيَ اللهُ عَنْهُ ، قَالَ: قَالَ رَسُولُ اللهِ صَلَّى اللهُ عَلَيْهِ وسَلَّمَ:

(يَا نِسَاءَ الْمُسْلِمَاتِ! لَا تَحْقِرَنَّ جَارَةٌ لِجَارَتِهَا وَلَوْ فِرْسِنَ شَاةٍ)

رَوَاهُ الْبُخَارِي ومُسْلِم.

Abu Hurairah, may Allah be pleased with him, said: The Messenger of Allah, peace be upon him, said:

(O Muslim women, never belittle any gift you give your neighbor, even if it is the hoof of a sheep)

[Al-Bukhari and Muslim].

[65] - الحَدِيثُ الخَامِسُ وَالسِّتُّون

عَنِ ابْنِ عُمَرَ ، رَضِيَ اللهُ عَنْهُمَا ، قَالَ: قَالَ رَسُولُ اللهِ صَلَّى اللهُ عَلَيْهِ وسَلَّمَ:

(لَنْ يَزَالَ الْمُؤْمِنُ فِي فُسْحَةٍ مِنْ دِينِهِ ، مَالَمْ يُصِبْ دَمًا حَرَامًا)

رَوَاهُ البُخَارِي.

Ibn `Umar, may Allah be pleased with them, said: The Messenger of Allah, peace be upon him, said:

(A believer continues to guard his faith (and thus hopes for Allah's Mercy) **as long as he does not shed blood unjustly)**

[Narrated by Al-Bukhari].

[66] - الحَدِيثُ السَّادِسُ وَالسِّتُّون

عَنِ ابْنِ مَسْعُودٍ ، رَضِيَ اللهُ عَنْهُ ، قَالَ: قَالَ رَسُولُ اللهِ صَلَّى اللهُ عَلَيْهِ وسَلَّمَ:

(سِبَابُ الْمُسْلِمِ فُسُوقٌ ، وَقِتَالُهُ كُفْرٌ)

رَوَاهُ الْبُخَارِي ومُسْلِم.

Ibn Mas-oud, may Allah be pleased with him, said: The Messenger of Allah, peace be upon him, said:

(Abusing a Muslim is Fusuq (an evil act) **and killing him is Kufur** (disbelief**))**

[Narrated by Al-Bukhari and Muslim].

[67] - الحَدِيثُ السَّابِعُ وَالسِّتُّون

عَنْ أَبِي هُرَيْرَةَ ، رَضِيَ اللهُ عَنْهُ ، قَالَ: سَمِعْتُ رَسُولَ اللهِ صَلَّى اللهُ عَلَيْهِ وسَلَّمَ يَقُولُ:

(قَالَ اللهُ تَعَالَى: أَنَا أَغْنَى الشُّرَكَاءِ عَنِ الشِّرْكِ ، مَنْ عَمِلَ عَمَلًا أَشْرَكَ فِيهِ مَعِي غَيْرِي ، تَرَكْتُهُ وشِرْكَهُ)

رَوَاهُ مُسْلِمٌ.

Abu Hurairah, may Allah be pleased with him, said: I heard the Messenger of Allah, peace be upon him, saying:

(Almighty Allah said: I am self-sufficient and in no need of having partners. He who does a thing for the sake of someone besides Me, I discard him and his polytheism)

[Narrated by Muslim].

[68] - الحَدِيثُ الثَّامِنُ وَالسِّتُّون

عَنْ عُثْمَانَ ، رَضِيَ اللهُ عَنْهُ ، قَالَ: قَالَ رَسُولُ اللهِ صَلَّى اللهُ عَلَيْهِ وَسَلَّمَ:

(مَـنْ مَاتَ وَهُوَ يَعْلَمُ أَنَّـهُ لا إِلَهَ إِلَّا اللهُ دَخَـلَ الْجَنَّـةَ)

رَوَاهُ مُسْلِمٌ.

Uthman, may Allah be pleased with him, said: The Messenger of Allah, peace be upon him, said:

(Whoever dies knowing there is no god has the right to be worshipped but Allah, he will enter Paradise)

[Narrated by Muslim].

[69] - الحَدِيثُ التَّاسِعُ وَالسِّتُون

عَنْ عَبْدِ اللهِ بْنِ عَمْرٍو بْنِ الْعَاصِ، رَضِيَ اللهُ عنْهُمَا ، قَالَ: قَالَ رَسُولُ اللهِ صَلّى اللهُ عَلَيْهِ وسَلَّمَ:

(اللَّهُمَّ مُصَرِّفَ الْقُلُوبِ صَرِّفْ قُلُوبَنَا عَلَى طَاعَتِكَ)

رَوَاهُ مُسْلِمٌ.

Abdullah ibn Amr ibn Al-Aas, may Allah be pleased with him, said: The Messenger of Allah, peace be upon him, said:

(O Allah, You control the hearts, direct our hearts to Your obedience)

[Narrated by Muslim].

[70] - الحَدِيثُ السَّبْعُون

عَنْ أَنَسٍ ، رَضِيَ اللهُ عَنْهُ ، قَالَ: كَانَ أَكْثَرُ دُعَاءِ النَّبِيِّ صَلَّى اللهُ عَلَيْهِ وسَلَّمَ:

(اللَّهُمَّ آتِنَا فِي الدُّنْيَا حَسَنَةً ، وَفِي الآخِرَةِ حَسَنَةً ، وَقِنَا عَذَابَ النَّارِ)

رَوَاهُ البُخَارِي ومُسْلِم.

Anas, may Allah be plessed with him, said: The Prophet, Peace be upon him, often in his supplication was saying:

(O Allah, give us which is good in this world and in the Hereafter, and protect us from the torment of the Fire)

[Narrated by Al-Bukhari and Muslim].

قَالَ اللهُ تَعَالَى:

(لَقَدْ كَانَ لَكُمْ فِي رَسُولِ اللهِ أُسْوَةٌ حَسَنَةٌ لِمَنْ كَانَ يَرْجُو اللهَ وَالْيَوْمَ الآخِرَ وَذَكَرَ اللهَ كَثِيرًا)

(There has certainly been for you in the Messenger of Allah an excellent example for anyone whose hope is in Allah and the Last Day and who remembers Allah often)

(33:21)

Index - الفهرس

Page No. رَقم الصّفحة Hadith No. رَقم الحَدِيثُ

Page No. رَقم الصّفحة Hadith No. رَقم الحَدِيثُ

Page No. رقم الصّفحة | Hadith No. رَقم الحَدِيثُ

Page No. رقم الصّفحة Hadith No. رَقم الحَدِيثُ

References - المَرَاجِع

صَحِيحُ البُخارِي

Sahih Al-Bukhari, (Arabic, English)
Translated by Dr. Muhammed Muhsin Khan

صَحِيحُ مُسْلِم

Sahih Muslim, (Arabic, English)
(Hafiz Abu Tahir Zubair, Ed., & Nasiruddin al-Khattab, Trans.)

شَرْح رِيَاض الصَّالِحِين

Commentary on the Riyad-us-Saliheen (Arabic, English) Volume1 and Volume 2
(Hafiz Salahuddin Yusuf, Ed., & Dr. Muhammad Amin, Trans.)

الْحَمْدُ لِلهِ الَّذِي بِنِعْمَتِهِ تَتِمُّ الصَّالِحَات

(Praise be to Allah, the One who by His favors good works are accomplished)

(صحيح الجامع - رقم 4640)